DIY Wedding Ideas.
Creative Decoration Projects for the Very Special Day!

Table of Contents

DIY Wedding Ideas:..1

Introduction..3

Chapter 1. Designing Your Wedding Invitations 5

Chapter 2. Setting the Right Mood with Your Wedding Decorations.......................................8

Chapter 3. DIY Wedding Table Decorations and Centrepieces...12

Chapter 4. DIY Wedding Ceremony Program Ideas..19

Chapter 5. DIY Wedding Favours...22

Conclusion 33

Introduction

First I would like to thank and congratulate you on downloading **"DIY Wedding: Amazing DIY Decoration Ideas for the Very Special Day!"** If you are a person that loves to create and design things then what better time to bring out your creative side than when you are putting together your wedding plans.

This is your special day in your life so why not make the things for your wedding using your own personal flare making this day truly your own. Think not only of the joy in getting married but also the pride you will feel when others compliment your beautiful designs and creations that you made for your wedding. These will be unique pieces that you cannot walk in and buy—because they are original made with your own two hands.

You take take the ideas and suggestions in this book and use them as a base—and your own special touch to them to make them truly your own. Just think there is not going to be another wedding in the whole world that is going to have the same identical decorations as your wedding—how wonderful is that?

In this book I will mention to you about purchasing kits and what you will have to do to put them together. If you want to make them right from scratch that too is an option because I will explain to you the entire process so that you can make items from scratch if you so desire.

I will offer you a list of materials, along with easy to follow step-by-step instructions to create various items by hand. You are going to find these projects so much fun and easy to do. You will have your guests in shock when you tell them that you made the decorations yourself for your wedding. I would suggest that you do not leave making items for your wedding to the last minutes.

It may take you a few tries to get things as you would like them to be. So make sure to give yourself ample time to put all the items together as you would like them. You even might want to ask your friends and family for some added help in making things for your wedding.

They would be more than happy to help out and make your special day the best it can be for you. This can be a great time to spend with the people that are in your wedding party also, it can be a great way to strengthen your bonds with them.

Chapter 1. Designing Your Wedding Invitations

One of the most important items in your wedding is your wedding invitations. They will give potential guests a first impression, and they are vital in setting the mood and tone of your wedding.

There are many different ways to make a wedding invite too many for me to name all of them. The ideas I have gathered here for wedding invitations are ones that you can use as a baseline for and you may add your own special touch to them to make them your own.

DIY Traditional Wedding Invitations.

If you want to go for a traditional look for your invitations than template for your programs and your more use the same invites.

You could choose to do a one-page type you may want to go for a booklet-like of invite or style of invite. In chapter for you will see program instructions, they are very similar to the below postcard instructions. All you have to do is to replace the schedule information with all of the proper event information and you are all set.

DIY Postcard Wedding Invitations.

You can use this way to give people a traditional paper invitation to your wedding adding a wonderful contemporary look to them. You can also save yourself some money here on the added expense of envelopes. Most basic postcards are about 3.5 inches by 5 inches.

You can easily do this yourself by designing in the Photoshop or any other program that is designed based on your computer software program. Doing this you will be able to setup the proper dimensions that you are looking for.

Choose a wonderful and dynamic picture to go on your postcard, that will grab the attention of those that view it. Since it is a wedding invite, I would like to suggest that you think about going with an engagement picture.

Whatever picture you and your partner decide to go with for your invites make sure that it is high-resolution enough that it will withstand printing. To do this process effectively you should set your DPI to at least 240. You want to keep in mind that one of the earmarks associated with a postcard is that it is colourful, bold, graphic, so keep this in mind when you are choosing your picture.

When you are setting your image decide if you would like it to have a border or not. If you are not sure than test a few borders out to see what you prefer. If you are going with a border use the ruler tool in Photoshop to make sure your border is the correct width and placement. Then in creating your graphics use layers. You may want to make it the same font as your programs and place settings so they all match nicely.

You do not want to clutter the front of your invite with no more than the general invite and greeting such as: "You are cordially invited to the wedding of (insert name) and (insert name)." Then you may choose to create a back or hand write it. If you decide that you are going to print it make sure that your printer will allow you to do a double-sided document. If you want to write it by hand then make sure that you include:

- date of wedding
- Time
- Location
- Dress Code
- RSVP
- Whether your guest is bringing a date or not

DIY Virtual Invitations. I personally feel that the paper invitations offer more of a classy flair. However, it might be a good idea to send an "evite" as people check their emails more frequently than their mailboxes. They will also receive the evite much faster than the paper invite that is going through the mail.

There is an assortment of places that you can go to pick out evite cards such as evite.com, punchbowl.com and greenvelope.com to name just a couple of them. On these sites you will find a great selection of wonderful templates for you to choose from. Sending evites as well as paper invitations will help ensure that all of your guests have received their invitations.

Chapter 2. Setting the Right Mood with Your Wedding Decorations

I love the decorations that I see at outdoor weddings, they are usually the most effective and lovely. However, if you are having an indoor wedding no worries there is plenty that you can do to decorate your indoor wedding to make it look amazing. I will be focusing more on summer weddings since this is the main time of year when weddings are held. And many of the ceremonies during this time of year are held outdoors. Some couples get married in a church and then have their reception at an outdoor venue. This of course will be something that you and your partner will decide while planning your special day.

DIY Daisy Chains. Of course for this you do not have to use daisies but use the flowers of your choice perhaps ones that match your wedding bouquet.

Materials you will need:

- scissors or an exacto knife
- flowers that still have the stems on them

Directions:

Make a slit on each flower stem that is about half-inch. Now pull the stem from one flower through the slit of another flower. You are just going to repeat this process until you reach the desired length of daisy or flower chain that you are seeking to make. At each end of the chain I would suggest that you link the ends to a strong robe or some kind of ribbon perhaps.

Choose a colour of ribbon that matches your wedding colours. Then you can take these flower chains and hang them from posts, trees, railings or on the backs of chairs for your ceremony. I think this is a much more lovelier look than flag garlands.

DIY Hanging Lanterns. I love the look of hanging lanterns especially at an outdoor wedding ceremony or celebration of some sort. You can get many different kinds of lanterns such as tin or paper made lanterns that you can place candles inside. There is even solar lanterns that look wonderful as well.

Try to go for lanterns that match the colours of your programs and wedding invitations. My husband got these lovely lanterns that we lit then we released them and they floated up into the air—I have to say I loved them and so did our guests. This what part of my own wedding plan that I had no idea about until they were brought forth to be lit—it was a nice surprise indeed! The thicker the paper for lanterns the better so the lantern will hold up nicely.

DIY Homemade Tin Lantern

material needed:

- markers

- a tin can

- crushed ice

- wire handle

- tea lights

Directions:

Clean the cans and draw a pattern you would like onto the outside of the cans using the markers. Fill the inside of can with crushed ice to prevent the can from denting while you are putting holes in it to make your special pattern. Remove the ice then add a wire handle. These will look great hanging from a tree. These are much more sturdier to use compared to paper lanterns especially if you are using real lit candles inside them. The sturdier the lantern the safer it will be.

DIY Fun Push-pop Confetti Holders. These are cheap and easy to make getting the supplies you will need at your local craft store. You can ask loved ones perhaps those in your bridal party to hand them out to others at your wedding.

Materials you will need to make push-pops confetti holders:

- kraft labels

- pop-up containers

- scissors

- tissue paper

Directions:

Make labels to wrap around your confetti-holders with perhaps nice cheerful sayings on them. Then cut up small pieces of tissue paper in your colours of choice and put them into the confetti containers and put the lid on them. Your guests will get fun out of using these during your wedding.

DIY Mr. and Mrs Chair Banner. To make this fun banner for the back of the new couples chairs you will be able to get the supplies you need at your local craft store.

Materials you will need to make banner:

- ribbon
- foam material
- hole-puncher
- glitter
- glue

Directions:

You can download a free template for your banner online. You can get foam material from craft store to cut out your letters from. Using the hole-puncher make holes in each end of letters to put the pieces of ribbon through to hold them in place.

Using glue cover the letters with glue and then apply the glitter of your choice. Once this has dried add the ribbons tying each end onto the back of the his and hers chairs of the bride and groom.

Chapter 3. DIY Wedding Table Decorations and Centrepieces

DIY Tea Lights Table Decorations. Using tea lights are a great basic form of light for an outdoor wedding ceremony or indoor. If you are concerned about a fire starting due to using tea lights you may choose to have battery powered tea lights instead. You can place the tea lights on top of your tables amongst tossed rose pedals as a nice decoration for the wedding tables. You do not have to use rose petals on your tables you may choose to scatter the pedals of another flower that you like.

DIY Floral Vial Place Cards. You may choose to  use plastic vials to cut down on the costs. You can get most of your supplies at your local craft store.

Materials needed for floral vial place cards:

- vial

- flowers

- kraft paper

- hole puncher

- twist ties

- fabric

- glue

Directions:

Choose a swatch of fabric that will match your chosen colours for your wedding. Glue onto the fabric the piece of kraft paper. Write the name of the guest on the kraft paper, use hole puncher to punch hole in the name tag. Put a twist tie through the hole and use it to secure the name tag to the floral vial place card.

DIY Rustic Centrepiece. Why not paint mason jars with pastel paints to give a real rustic appearance to your wedding. These are cheap and easy to put together giving a lovely affect to your wedding reception tables.

Materials you will need for rustic centrepiece:

- pastel paint
- mason jars
- flowers
- sandpaper
- twine

Directions:

Paint the mason jars and allow for the paint to dry. Then take the sandpaper and lightly sand the jars to give them that rustic-looking appearance. Add your choice of flowers to the jars. Take some twine and tie around the top of the jars.

DIY Paint-dipped Cork Place-card Holder. These are a quick and easy way to make some wonderful place-card holders for your tables. You can get corks at your local craft store.

Materials you will need to make paint-dipped cork place-card holders:

- choice of paint
- corks
- exacter knife

Directions:

You need to cut a slit at one end of the cork for the card to be placed in. On the other end of the cork you will dip this end in the paint of your choice.

DIY Vintage Wooden Round Table Numbers. If you are having an outdoor wedding these rustic-looking table numbers would work great for you. You can get your supplies for this project (including the wooden discs) at your local craft store.

Materials you will need to make vintage table numbers:

- woodburner

- wooden discs or rounds

- flowers of your choice

Directions:

You first will use the wood burner to burn into each disc or wood round a number of a table. This will give you a lovely look to your outdoor wedding that is so easy to put together but has a great affect with adding a nice touch to the ambiance of your wedding. Place some flowers lying across the round to add to the affect of the display.

DIY Cork Name Card Place Setting.

These simple cork settings are easy and inexpensive to make. You can get the corks and paper from your local craft store.

Materials you will need for cork name card place setting:

- corks

- coloured cardstock paper

- pins

- flowers of your choice

- twine or ribbon

- hole-puncher

Directions:

Take your flower tops and place on top of the cork, keep in place using a pin. Write out guest names on cardstock paper, cut away one corner on an angle. On the opposite corner use hole-puncher to make a hole. Then put a piece of twine or ribbon through the hole and tie to the cork.

DIY Mint Sprig Name Place Table Setting.

These settings are so quick and easy to make.

Materials you need to make a mint sprig name place table setting:

- brown name tags

- white marker

- sprig of fresh mint

Directions:

Take the name tags and write the names of your guests on them using the white marker. In the hold on the name tags insert a small sprig of fresh mint and place on top of napkin on plate.

DIY Pebbles Name Place Settings. This is a fun idea to use especially if you are having your wedding near a beach. Use simple pebbles that you can collect from the beach writing your guests names onto the pebbles using a white marker.

Materials you will need:

- pebbles

- white marker

Directions:

Clean off the pebbles and allow to dry and use a fine white tip marker to write the names of your guest on each pebble.

DIY Apple Name Place Setting.

This is a great name setting to use especially if you are getting married on a farm or having an outdoor wedding. Put a simple name tag made of cardstock paper with guests name on it across the front of an apple. Tie some twine around the apple to hold the name tag in place.

DIY Seashell Name Place Settings.

This is a great idea to use if you are having a beach wedding. Collect an assortment of small seashells or you can purchase them at craft store near you.

Materials you will need:

- seashells

- cardstock paper for name tags

- glue

- download a free name tag templates

Directions:

Download a free name tag template and use this to make your name place cards. Glue on to each card a seashell in one corner.

DIY Heart Shaped Name Place Settings.

You can get creative here as you do not have to stick with the heart shape but perhaps you might prefer to go with a butterfly or bird. Cut your shape of choice out with a slit on it so you can use this to attach it to the guests wine glass.

Chapter 4. DIY Wedding Ceremony Program Ideas

Fun Brightly Coloured DIY Felt Program Holders. These fun and easy to put together felt program bags you can make with a few supplies that you can get from your local craft store.

Materials you will need to make felt program holders:

- bright colours of felt

- glue

- twine

Directions:

You can cut out the size of cloth you want not too big to make a small rectangular square pouch applying glue along edges of pouch. Fold over cloth to make your pouch cut a piece of twine to use as handle and glue the ends of twine at either side of the pouch. Place your wedding programs inside the pouches and hang on the back of chairs for your guests.

DIY Cedar Twigs Programs. Add to your programs a piece of cedar twig especially if you are doing an outdoor wedding. This will give off a nice aroma and will look great with the outdoor setting for your wedding. It is simple to put together all you need to do is to weave a twig of cedar into your wedding program leave on the seats of guests. You can also use this when making your place settings as shown in the picture below.

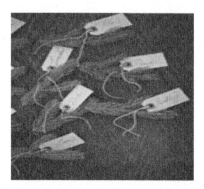

DIY One-page Scroll Wedding Program.

You can make up a lovely scroll design wedding program choose from many of the free templates online to create your scroll design. You can either have someone hand them out to people as they arrive or you can simply place a scroll on each seat at the wedding.

DIY Accordion Fold Wedding Program.

You can choose for a large assortment of programs designs that you can find online that you can download for free. Choose a nice cardstock paper and you will have your wedding programs in no time!

DIY Tie **Pages of Wedding Program with Ribbon.** This design you can get from an assortment of free downloads to choose from.

Materials you need:

- cardstock paper
- hole-puncher
- ribbon or twine
- free downloaded  templates

Directions:

Once you have chosen the templates that you want to use for your wedding program print them out onto good cardstock paper. Using a hole-puncher punch holes in one top corner of each card that is going to be included in your wedding program. Then using ribbon/twine, string through holes to attach each card.

DIY Folded Wedding Program Tied with Ribbon. After you have chosen a nice free template for wedding program design fold it and hold it closed by tying a ribbon around it. These you can place on the chairs for the guests to pick up when they are ready to sit.

Chapter 5. DIY Wedding Favours

DIY Edible Barbeque Rub Wedding Favours. These are so easy and cheap to put together and are just perfect for those outdoor weddings. You can make your own little labels and buy the containers at a craft store and decorative string or ribbon to tie around bottles. And pic up the barbeque rub at your local grocery store.

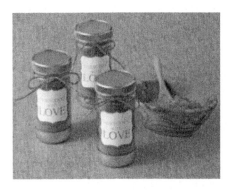

DIY Pine Cone Fire Starter for a Wedding Favour. These make a great wedding favour especially for winter weddings or outdoor weddings.

DIY Its A Match Wedding Favour. This is a cute and easy to put together wedding party favour. You can get some nice little jars and lids at craft store. Get some free downloads of labels for jars. And fill them with some matches and you will light up the room with smiling faces!

DIY Mini Terrarium Wedding Favour. This is a cute and easy favour to put together that is a gift that your guests can admire long after your wedding.

You can get most of the supplies you will need at your local craft store. You might want to visit your local garden nursery to get the plants you want. You can make your display stick labels by downloading a free template.

DIY Flip-flops for Wedding Favours. Giving flip-flops at a wedding favour works very well at outdoor weddings especially those that are happening on a beach. If you are really organized you can try and figure out how many of each size of flip-flop you will need. You can tie little thank you tags to them, and you can choose to download a free template to use for the tags.

DIY Cookies in Mason Jars for Wedding Favours. These are a wedding favour that you know your guests will enjoy munching on at some point. Fill mason jars with a cookie of your choice perhaps even a mixed selection. Make labels for mason jars using a free template that you can download from online. And for an added touch you may want to wrap a ribbon around the jars or a bit of twine.

DIY Lottery Tickets for Wedding Favours. These are fun wedding favours to give that your guests will enjoy and they are easy to put together. Just choose a nice envelope that will suit your wedding colours and write on the front "For Richer For Poorer" and glue a penny under the word poorer.

DIY Sand and Seashells in a Bottle Wedding Favours. This is a great idea if you are getting married on a beach and you want your guest to take home a memento of this you can bottle some seashells and sand in cute little bottles. Make nice labels for them using a free template that you can download online. Tie a bit of twine around bottle perhaps have a seashell charm on the string.

DIY Tulip Bulbs for Wedding Favours. Place some tulip bulbs in little boxes of your choice of colour and wrap with matching ribbon. You may want to add a small thank you tag on the box.

DIY Wildflower Seeds for Wedding Favours. Use tiny envelopes to place some wildflower seeds into them for your guests. Add a nice thank you tag using a free template that you can download from online. You may also want to wrap it in a nice bow.

DIY Recycled Cardboard Wrap for Wedding Favours. If you are someone that loves to recycle then why not use recycled cardboard to wrap your wedding favours in. This is very inexpensive all you need is some recycled cardboard, twine, and make some labels using a free template that you can download from online or make them yourself.

DIY Make Homemade Soaps for Wedding Favours.

You can purchase all you need to make homemade soaps at your local craft store. You can purchase soap making kits at craft stores. Tie a bit of twine around them adding a thank you tag to them.

DIY Personalized Matchboxes For Wedding Favours. You can make your own personalized matchbox labels using a free template that you can download from online and a cardstock paper. Have you and your partners names on the matchbox labels. You can simply make the labels and glue them over the top of the matchboxes.

DIY Box of Cherries for Wedding Favours. This would make a great wedding favour for a wedding that is being held outdoors. Can make labels for boxes using a free template that you can download online and then just glue them to the outside of cherry boxes.

DIY Individual Mint Pack for Wedding Favour. This is a cheap and easy wedding favour to put together. Add label on packet of mint with the saying on it "_____ (bride) & ____(groom) Mint to Be." This is a cute wedding favour that is very easy to put together with little to no fuss.

DIY Hugs & Kisses Wedding Favour. This is a great DIY wedding favour, all you need is a mason jar, ribbon, label that you can use free template by downloading online to make, glitter, glue and of course some yummy Hershey kisses. Take the lid of the mason jar and put glue on it then sprinkle your desired colour of glitter allow to dry. Place Hershey kisses into jar, wrap with ribbon around jar, and add personalized label.

DIY Sunflower Seed Packet for Wedding Favour.
Easy and fun to make, just glue a packet of sunflower seeds
onto a Popsicle stick, these you can purchase at local craft
store. Then you can find a creative way to display them
such as below—placing a sign that instructs your
guests to take one and also says "Watch Love
Grow." This idea will work really well with an
outdoor summer or fall wedding.

DIY Popcorn in a Mason Jar for a Wedding Favour. This is a fun Wedding favour that
would work great at a summer or fall wedding. All you need is some popcorn kernels, mason
jars, twine, paper to cover lid, and personalized labels that you can make using free template
online, and some cardstock paper.

Add the fun words "Thanks for Popping By" on the label!

DIY Love Bug Wedding Favour. This is a fun and sweet  wedding favour that is easy to put together and cheap to make. Cut the shape of Mason jar out of cardstock paper with window hole in the middle. Attach on the back of it a bag of jelly worms. Write the words "Love Bug" on front of jar and a thank you from the bride and groom.

DIY Spoonful of Kisses Wedding Favour. All you need is a spoon, some Hershey kisses, plastic or net wrap, ribbon, and personalized labels.

DIY Mint Tic Tacs for Wedding Favour. This is an easy
a n d simple wedding favour to put together. All you need to do
is to make your own personalized labels can put words on "Simply Mint to Be Together" and
the bride and grooms names. Glue these labels onto your tic tac containers.

DIY Paper bag of Strawberries for Wedding Favour. We all love strawberries, they
will be a big hit at a summer wedding as a party favour. All you have to do is to get some
paper bags from craft store or dollar store, make some personalized labels using free template

you can download online and fill with strawberries. This is a yummy wedding favour that many of your guests will enjoy!

Conclusion

I hope that this collection of ideas and tips for helping you to plan your special day will give you some ideas that you can build from to create something special that is uniquely your own. Often times it can help us to get our creative juices flowing when we see some ideas of others, we can then use these as a base to build from.

Adding your own special flare to your wedding details is what will make it your own—and there isn't a better day than your wedding day to make it into your special day, without spending a fortune to do so. These DIY tips and suggestions will not only save you money on the expense of your wedding but quite simply they will be projects that you and your loved ones will really have fun putting together.

I wish you all the best in your life and may you have the dream wedding you want! I am sure once you get those creative juices flowing you will even surprise yourself on the ideas that you will come up with for your wedding! Of course the most important thing is that you are marrying the person that you have chosen as your life partner—this is what makes your wedding a special day indeed! Congratulations and all the best to you and your life partner!

FREE Bonus Reminder

If you have not grabbed it yet, please go ahead and download your special bonus report *"DIY Projects. 13 Useful & Easy To Make DIY Projects To Save Money & Improve Your Home!"*

Simply Click the Button Below

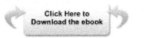

OR **Go to This Page**
http://diyhomecraft.com/free

BONUS #2: More Free & Discounted Books

Do you want to receive more Free & Discounted Books?

We have a mailing list where we send out our new Books when they go free or with a discount on Kindle. Click on the link below to sign up for Free & Discount Book Promotions.

=> Sign Up for Free & Discount Book Promotions <=

OR Go to this URL

http://zbit.ly/1WBb1Ek

Printed in Great Britain
by Amazon

79403037R00031